Failure to Make Round Rotis

Failure to Make Round Rotis

Poems on
rebellion, resilience
and relationships

MEHAK GOYAL

JUGGERNAUT BOOKS
C-I-128, First Floor, Sangam Vihar, Near Holi Chowk,
New Delhi 110080, India

First published by Juggernaut Books 2023

10 9 8 7 6 5 4 3 2 1

P.–ISBN: 9789353451660
E–ISBN: 9789353451684

Book designed by Meena Rajasekaran
Illustrations by Shikhar Gaur
Additional typesetting support by R. Ajith Kumar

Printed at Thomson Press India Ltd

For my family.

For those who feel the urge to overcompensate
for their failure to make round rotis.

‘The knowledge of cooking does not come pre-installed in a vagina.’

Chimamanda Ngozi Adichie

‘Poetry is the way we help give name to the nameless so it can be thought.’

Audre Lorde

– Contents –

– Prologue –

Ice Lolly Recipe

Remove a frozen memory
Cover it with a clean cloth
Hammer it with hoarded rage and guilt
Fill a paper cup with the crushed fiasco
Insert a wooden stick of resilience
Place and press more numb fragments till they console each other
Remove the first draft from the cup carefully
Pour colourful metaphors until soaked
Sprinkle feminist masala for extra punch
Slurp it loudly
Consume it cold
May it soothe your sweltering soul

Medal of Participation

Fly

The giant wings halt
opposite the transparent wall.
'Mummy, will THAT take us to nani?'
She nods.

'Mummy, but there are
no eagles or brooms.
How will we fly
to the door?'

'I will provide the magical stairs
till you learn to fly, bulbul.'
She wraps me in her arms
and carries me to the plane.

Privilege

Jump. Stretch. Reach.
My fingertips graze the green skin
of the obstinate mango.
'Next time,' I taunt
before heading home.

I look at the tree from the
balcony of my house.

Another girl, dressed in a
turquoise frock, points
to my mango. The king lifts
his princess, her hands
pull what was mine.

Her loud laughter
is planted in my mind.

Report Card

A: Kiss on the cheek, hug, Baskin-Robbins

B: Pat on the head, do better

C: Lock in dark bathroom

D: Smack soft skin

E: Hurl slipper

F: Hostel

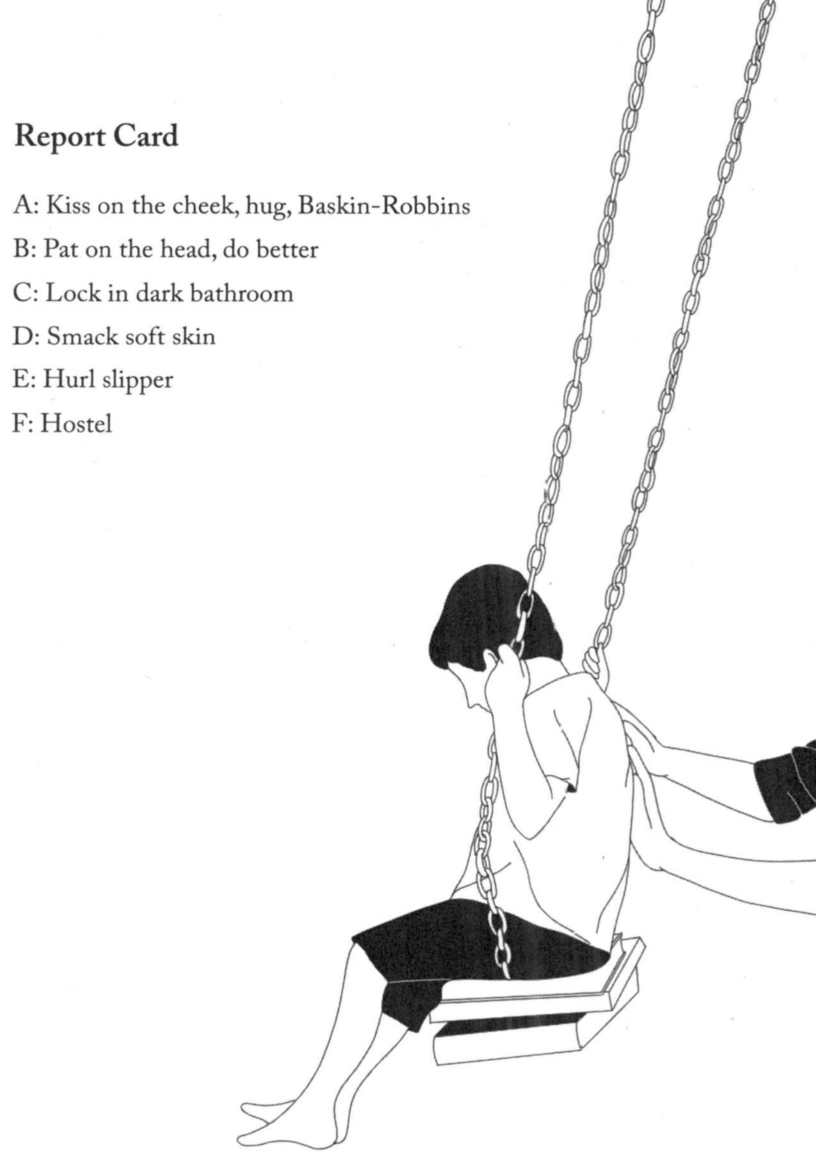

Exam Boards

'Ma'am, please.
Five more minutes, please.'
My tears blot the ink.

She pulls my answer sheet so
forcefully that her body
falls through the window.

She lands on her paws –
a ferocious black cat,
eyes red, racing towards me.

Her claws aim for my face.
6 a.m. My alarm rings.
I feel the crescent moon and

small star scratched
on my forehead.
I look in my mirror. C+.

I rush for my next exam.
A heavy iron watch cuffs
my wrist. 'Drop your pen

when asked. Would be a shame
to snap this delicate thing.'
She laughs. The bell rings. I write.

Reading

A mango's skin
peeled lightly, carefully.

An oil container
dehydrated of its contents.

A bag of wheat
dusted of its last grain.

All its words
poured, preserved
in my mind –

I hum my book –
my anthem,
until the next one.

First Prize

Late evening, I reach home
after tennis practice carrying
my trophy close to my chest.

Radha opens our door.
'Where are Mama and Papa?' I ask,
not finding their Toyota outside.

'They are having dinner with friends.
Come! You must be hungry. I made
your favourite – Rajma chawal.'

My trophy tucked like a teddy bear in my bed,
I force my eyes to stay open, but in vain.
Next morning, Radha makes halwa to celebrate

while my parents rush for their morning jog.
My school bus honks. I stare at my golden cup
one last time, its gleam not reaching my eyes.

Medal of Participation

I held my
medal of participation
after my five-hundred metre race
in my sweaty palms,
beaming with pride.

My parents cheered
for me loudly.
We would
eat ice cream
and celebrate.

It was a big day.

How to Lose Gracefully

'Out,' I call.

My opponent runs over to my side,
points with her racquet,
'No, the ball was in, see this mark.'

I am losing 5-3. Matchpoint.

'My side, my call. It was OUTSIDE the line.'
'Cheater,' she calls back.
Reflexively, I throw the ball at her.

The lie bounces from her racquet and brushes my face.
It hurts less than my incompetence.
She wins the next point. Match.

I raise my racquet to hit the ground.
My mother is looking at me. I pause midway.
Grabbing my tennis kit, I drag myself to the car.

'You will go back and shake hands.'
'NO.'
'Okay, we are not leaving then.'

Stomp. Stomp.
She doesn't love me at all.
Why is she taking her side?

Why is she making me do this?
This is worse than the horror that I just faced.
Stomp. Stomp.

'Hey, I forgot to shake hands.'
We do.
I turn back to run away.

She stops me. 'Listen, you really
played well today. It was a good match.'
I am smiling when I reach my car.

My mother stops at my favourite dessert shop.
'This victory calls for a chocolate bomb.
You earned it. I am so proud of you.'

Relatives

Clothes pile up in my closet.

Twin shirts arrive.
No more space.

I open my cupboard,
scan through it,
unable to find anything
cool and comforting
for a hot summer day.

Bully

I.

'Your boots are ugly –
just like your face,'
she snaps.

I am drinking water next to the cooler.

My throat gulps.
My heart protests.
My lips part.

Blinks later, I hear laughter from her audience.

II.

A week elapses.
Their thunderous laughter
strikes intermittently.

Retorts refuse
to form phrases as
thoughts ghost my tongue.

My beautiful brown boots
stare at me, 'How could you
not stand up for us?'

I shut my closet–
hoping to wear
my confidence soon.

III.

'Your opinions don't matter to me.'
I rehearse in the mirror.

My body clenches,
unable to carry its weight.

My words shiver,
unable to carry their meaning.

IV.

The predator studies the
solitary butterfly from afar –
imagining her palms clasping it.

I am washing my hands.
A foot taps.
She comments on my

usefulness or lack thereof
as a human in society.
This time I smile and say,

'That was really mean.
Does that make you feel
better about yourself?'

Her minions stare into silence.
The honed wings of the butterfly
cut the palms of the predator.

My boots carry me to sociology.

Water Bottle

Parched, they walk up to me –

sip, take notes,
slurp, suggestion,
gulp, gulp, favour.

I am left at the corner of the stairs,
forgotten and empty.

Friendship

The chocolate settled easily in
the palms of my peers
its shiny wrapper opened
like secret messages,
birthday invitations
and BFF wristbands,
stacked carefully later
in their backpacks.

Starving,
craving,
expecting
one M&M,
I found an unlimited
pack of Lindt bars.
Filling cavities,
not creating them.

The Fall

Astonished yet curious
they point,
suppressing smiles
as I am pushed off the ledge.
I am falling.

A scandalous act today.
Maybe worth a tweet tomorrow.
They stare at me
as I lie there motionless
bleeding on the ground.

They're spectators. Don't call them friends.

My Crowned Childhood

Tilt the gas cylinder horizontally.
Roll it on the floor.
Rotis cooked.
Dairy Milk devoured.

Embellish the rips
of my backpack with
Gryffindor pins and stickers.
A wand keyring rewarded.

A bucket of lukewarm water.
Ration for washing
body and long hair.
Shampoo doesn't burn eyes.

Sip lime water from the
reused Coke bottle.
Pretend you're sipping cola.
No glasses to clean.

No fingerprints, turmeric stains,
or pen markings
on the book borrowed.
Another one promised.

Handle the bright red trackpoint
on dad's laptop as delicately
as glass crockery when serving guests.
His sandal stays on the floor.

My favourite –
pick one dress from cousin's
wardrobe. Twirl like a princess.
Lock it in my cupboard.

My childhood
crowned with games.

The Couch

Our
chestnut coloured comfortable couch –
a three seater,
reading, TV, siesta.

Threads askew from
stitching our wounds.
A wobbly leg supported
by a cardboard cutout.
Cushions flattened by
the weight of our memories.
Chafed leather reflecting
its devotion and endurance.
A few scars hidden
like pencils in the folds.

Still
it refused to crumble,
just like us.

Adulting

My Façade

Week 1:

At first, *it* feels like an
itchy woollen sweater
against my skin.

I remove *it* as soon
as I reach home,
pretending not to notice

the red marks *it* leaves.
The loathing is mutual.
Maybe *it* will turn to satin soon.

Week 2:

Invitations to parties are more frequent,
like the lies told to my parents.

My fake laughs escape my throat smoothly.
My dull eyes glow with mascara and glitter.

A couple of girls roll their eyes
as novel fingers caress my palms.

It has gripped me like a bodycon dress,
not stripped off even when I sleep.

Week 3:

'You never had to fake
your smiles with us.'
My old friends stare, trying to
collect bits of me that are lost.

It rips. Their words find my skin.
'You are just jealous.'
It holds my spine straight.
I escape to class.

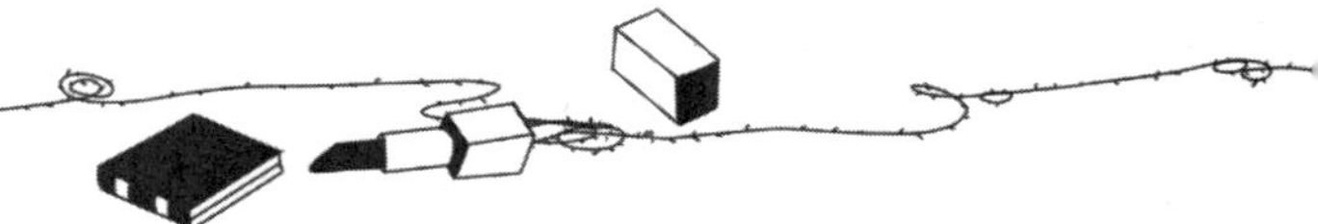

Week 4:

At home, my parents are planning
dinner at my favourite restaurant.

Before I can nod, he texts:
Party at Tanya's. Waiting for you outside.

My smile disappears. My stomach spins.
I rush to my room. Bury a playsuit in my bag.

Carrying textbooks in my arm,
'I have an important physics project

due tomorrow. Maybe next week?'
I leave my parents teary-eyed, trembling.

Maybe that is the price of belonging.
It is glued to my skin, unwilling to peel off.

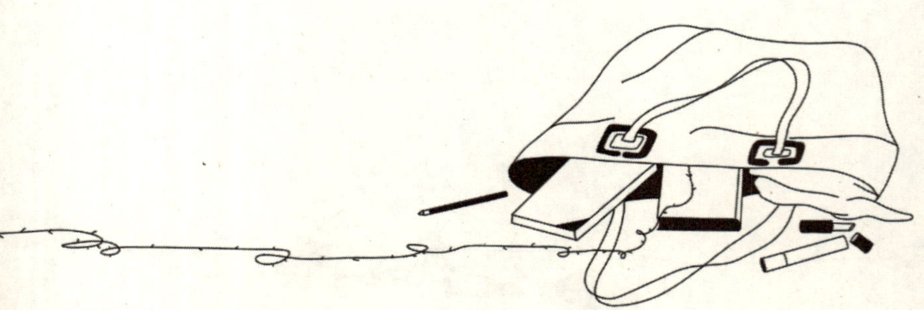

Result Card

D is for Dolce & Gabbana
she wanted written across
her small breasts instead of GAP.

D is for disappointment.
Her friends enjoyed
drink, spin the bottle, make out.
She chugged
physics, chemistry, maths.
Yet, failed miserably.

D is for depression
that devours her body,
kissing her tenderly from head to toe.

D is for don't,
the last thing she heard
her mother shout as she jumped.
She didn't have wings.
She couldn't fly.

D is for dreams
that trickle away
like her blood on
the cold concrete floor.

Parent and Child

The sun rises.
The sunflower sprouts.
Let's call it birth.

The sun struts.
The sunflower follows faithfully.
Let's call it childhood.

The sun shifts.
The sunflower yields hesitatingly.
Let's call it adolescence.

The sun summons.
The sunflower assertively faces east.
Let's call it graduation.

Let's call it nature.

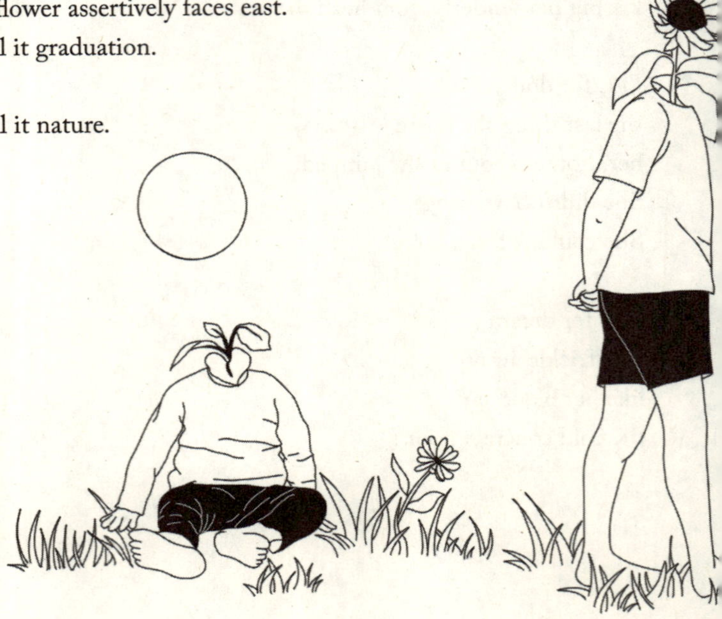

Adulting

The trumpeting horns
mixed with shrill curses
might help me vent my frustration.

The prolonged work hours meshed
with mandatory corporate events might help me
forget the real laughs I shared with friends.

The accidental shoulder rubs
on a crammed commute
might make me feel less lonely.

My 'social' drinking and smoking
might just provide the intoxicating
carelessness I crave.

My orchestrated photos
of airport hops and rooftop restaurants
might convince me I made it in life.

The smallness of my 1 BHK
apartment – the place I call home –
might help me unsee its emptiness.

Sirens

Window: Look, your porch swing calls.
Ukulele: Tune me, play me. Please.
Brownie: You're the only one who can see me, where did you go?
Harry Potter tiffin box: Take me to work.
Strawberry lip gloss: Remember our first kiss?
Bed: Hide, no one will seek you here.
Uno: Help! I am trapped in a drawer.
Teddy bear: Hold me.
Scrabble: Spell 'missing'.
Park: Did you bring the chalk for hopscotch?
Stairs: Climb me, I promise I won't let you fall.
Darkness: You aren't scared anymore! Shall I call thunder?
June: Let's take a vacation?

I listen to their banter,
when my phone rings –
back to work.

The Start-up

I.

I was adamant to plunge into
the stinging sea of start-ups –
the unforgiving waters
that promised prestige.

Sink or swim,
walking on dry land
leashed to my job
was just deplorable.

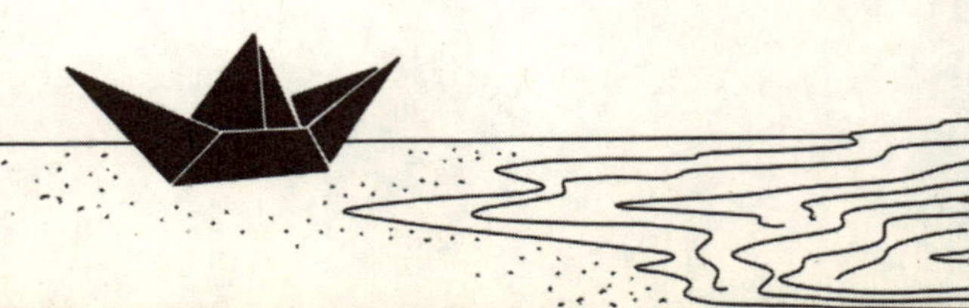

II.

After my idea kept me afloat in a nearby pond,
I dipped my trembling toe in the sea
that was specked with other dreamers.

I asked for space to wade through –
no acknowledgement, no pauses.
My requests turned to begs.

I punched, poked,
clawed and cursed.
My bleeding limbs fed the

thirsty sea as water lapped
around my calves,
I had anchored.

III.

Gunshot fired.
My first race began.

Veterans cut through water
like lightning in the sky.

A few parents tied a secret
engine around their child's waist.

Covert groups pushed their teammates
forward, others were kicked.

The finish line still a few
skills away from me, the race finished.

No participation trophies.
My despair, my reward.

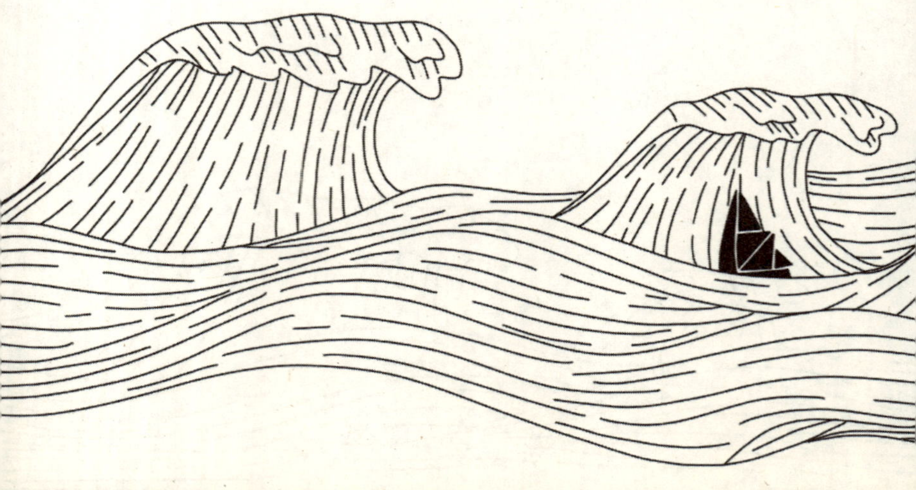

IV.

More races, more months.
A team formed. Techniques stocked.
Quicker strokes. Held breaths.

More races, more months.
Water gulped. Water coughed.
First to grab the rope.

Tears glistened on my body.
No applause. No cheers.
No triumphant music. No confetti.

Muscles aching. Gasping for breath.
Swallowing joy. Chasing deadlines.
I dive into the water again.

V.

A strong wave crashed.
My feet flapped to find the floor.
My drowning voice called out for help.

Blackness engulfed me
slowly, lovingly, like a
dark night eating a dying sun.

An investment angel
threw me a life ring,
dragged me back on board.

Saved from failure's rocking cradle,
we might just stay afloat longer.
We have to.

VI.

There were days we swam through the largest waves.
There were days we were knocked out despite wearing life vests.

There were days we swam against the current.
There were days we gave up.

There were days we won.
There were days we were clueless.

I walked back one step at a time –
a weekend with family,
reading ten minutes a day,
a drink with friends,
a smile here and a laugh there.

The trick:
tame the wave,
if you can't,
brave the untamed.

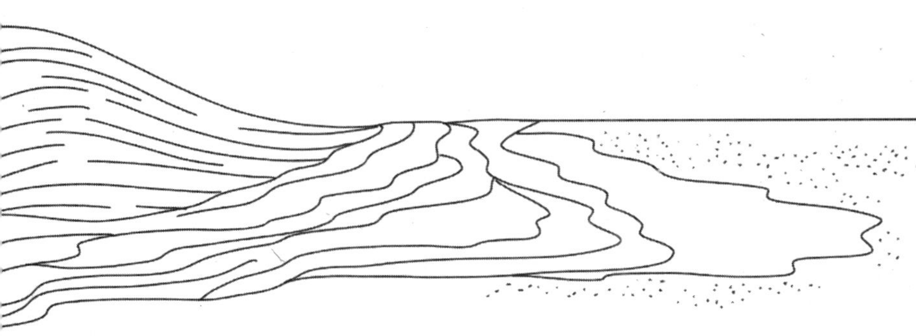

Lullaby

Listening to *Becoming* on Audible,
I travel back to my childhood room –

My head rested in my mother's lap,
'*The Famous Five* by Enid Blyton.
Chapter Two – "The Strange Cousin".'

'Mummy, I have short hair.
I can swim as fast as a boy.
I don't like playing with dolls.
Am I strange? Should I have a boy's name?'

'No, Rosebud, don't you see there's
a whole chapter dedicated to you?
You are going to bloom
no matter where you are planted.'

She continued reading the chapter.

Her voice plays like a
lullaby in my ears.
I sleep like a child in her mother's lap,
my AirPods slip out.

She

She radiates warmth
like an oil heater.
I inhale deeply, my body unclenches.

She makes me feel secure
like a precious coin
tucked in a sturdy wallet.

She adds colour
like a bouquet of roses, orchids and lilies
kept in the centre of a white room.

She fixes me
like a trained chef
does a ruined dish.

She never judges me
unlike a weighing scale
does a chocolate in my hand.

She holds me together
like diamond laces do
a Converse shoe.

She absorbs my negativity
like a high GSM towel
sops up heavy sweat.

She pushes me to
be my best version like an
architect fights for his building.

She sacrifices her needs
to fulfil mine
like a tree for humanity.

She made me
who I am.
I love you, Mom.

Opinions

My mother advised the
nourishing merry berry lip balm –
comforting, caring and complimenting.
It will never overpower you. Yet will make you shine.

My best friend recommended
longwear, smudge-proof pink lip stain –
dependable and trustworthy.
It stays with you even after a long exhausting day.

Another friend suggested
that I try and test samples.
Why devote your life to a single lip colour?

My cousin pointed at
the glossy devilish red lip crayon –
a charming coveted colour.
You will turn heads at every party.

My colleague endorsed
the rich plum shade
that befits a queen.
Why slog when you can rule?

Another acquaintance
whined and wailed –
my mother forced me to wear matte fuschia –
she said I couldn't be colourless anymore.

What did I get?
What *I* wanted.

A Letter to My Friends

Don't demand joy
when you
reflect nothing
but sadness.

Don't expect
understanding
when all you hurl is
anger and contempt.

Don't steal
love and affection
when you can offer
only indifference.

Friends

A few red sole pumps.
Pretty. Delicate. Studded.
Parties. Drinks. Stories on Instagram.
The weekend whirls by.
Afterwards, my wallet refuses to replenish
and blisters take weeks to heal.
Hazy names. Hazier faces.

A few tennis shoes.
Frowned on at a party.
Unwelcome at work.
Available only thrice a week.
for a quick game.
Sweat trickles down my back.
I am exhausted.

One slip-on shoe.
Cushions my fall.
Stretches to wrap me.
We are inseparable.
Dance. Library. Work. Workout. Theatre.
Spring. Summer. Fall. Winter.
No limping. No tripping. No slipping.
I take lighter steps.

A Gossip Column

Guess who I ran into
at the house party yesterday?
______ from school, you know,

ugly Betty? She was wearing
this tragic tangerine top. Ew!
She isn't 'fat' anymore, but her

black glasses were. Get contacts! Sheesh!
BUT OMG! Her boyfriend is DElicious.
She had a YSL bag on her shoulder.

Didn't look like a fake! Maybe he gifted it.
Writers don't earn that much, do they?
But honestly, what did he see in HER –

the girl who was dumped on a text
just before prom. Still, she attended,
ALONE. Oh God, what a shame!

Darn it.
I feel so terrible talking
like this. Maybe it's the wine.

Crystal clink.
Smiles stifle.
Conclusion circulates.

Another drink.
Another name.
Another party.

Rich

An expensive imported pencil
can't scrawl words
you don't have
out of your soul
on to precious handmade paper.

How to Be a Writer

Nowhere to run or hide,
I peel the nude bandage of
indifference that has merged with my skin.
Unstitch the sewn thread
carefully, one loop at a time.
Dig my long nails into
wilfully forgotten wounds.

Blood ebbs.
Fill an empty wine bottle.

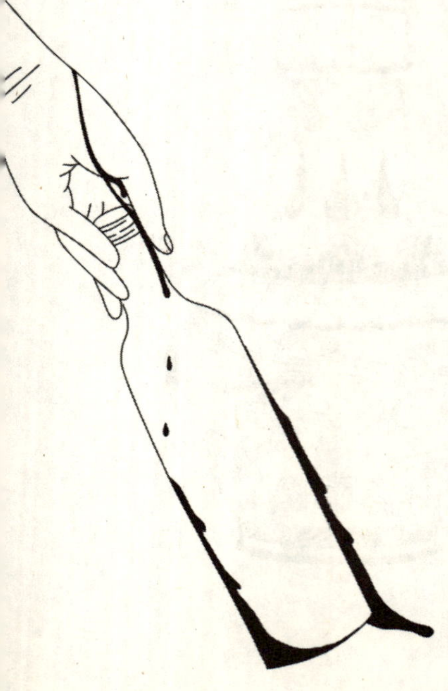

To the Reader

Open the bottle.
Let it breathe.
Sniff its calming aroma.
Sip my words.
Let their fruity flavour
linger on your tongue
till you can feel my heartbeat
reverberating with yours.

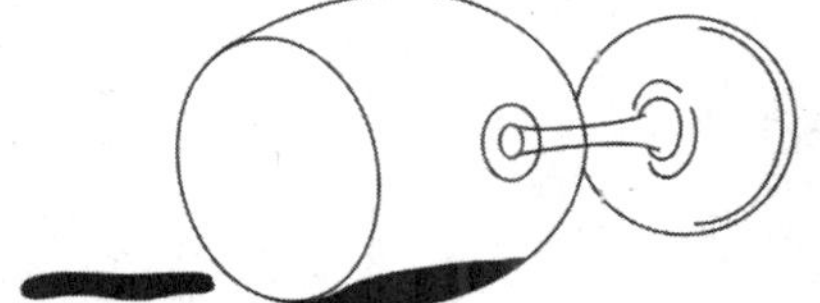

The Bottle of Promises

A Restaurant Monologue

He's only ten minutes late.
Probably stuck at work.

Time will fly when he's here.
Can't believe I found him on Bumble.

Let me text him?
No, let's wait five more minutes.

Watch. WINE.

Stop playing with the cutlery.
Stop rolling the napkin.

Will he like what I'm wearing?
Why is my heart racing?

Smile.
A little less.

Shall I get another glass, Ma'am?

Don't freeze!
Nod.

Phone. Instagram –
Even SHE has a boyfriend.

Twenty minutes.
Shall I call him now?

Will I look desperate?
Am I DESPERATE?

Watch. WINE.

A chocolate ice-cream tub.
Takeaway, Ma'am?

Hands – stop trembling.
Bill – leave a tip.
Mind – don't see the happy couple.
Tears – wait.
Heels – walk like a lady.

But he seemed so genuine.
Can't believe I found HIM on Bumble.

Punching the car steering doesn't help.
Crying on the way back home doesn't help.

Spoon. Tub.
Crazy, stupid, love.

Oh Ryan, why can't all guys be
like you're with Emma?

The Bestseller

We meet at a bookstore.

An enticing cover,
a promising preface,
could be a thrilling story.

We walk back to my apartment.
I enter my room.
I lie down, the book beside me.

Covers removed.
The first chapter is a drag.
The second strained.

I pretend to enjoy
the remaining tricks,
hoping for a plot twist.

My smile fades.
My interest walks out.
Frivolous finish.

A short read.
Shall I rate
on Goodreads?

Never again will I
judge a book
by its cover.

Swimming Pool

Conforming to his moods
and schedule, I am his
personal swimming pool.

He dives inside me.
My coolness envelops him.
'You're a blessing on a hot summer day,'

he says, coming out for air.
He plunges again–
strokes quicker

until he has finished.
His body leaves me.
'Another lap?' I splash.

'Work is hectic.'
He walks out, takes a
quick shower, changes clothes.

'Tomorrow, then?' I bubble.
'I'll call you.'
Typing on his phone, he departs.

I turn blue.

Garden

Our love was once
a blooming garden,
wafting joy.

But now the flowers wilt.
Quarrels, like insects,
swarm about.
The bees of happiness
have long forsaken us.
Memories, like broken bottles,
are strewn around.
Cacti of regret
flourish by the gate.

If only we had planted new seeds
when the old blossoms were dying.

The Bottle of Promises

Don't take a sip –
I intoxicate.

Don't drink me –
the hallucinations
of a happily ever after will
cloud your discontent.

When you wake up
your head will hurt.
Your stomach will clench in pain.
You will be hung-over.

Don't. Please.
Please. Don't.

Oh dear. What a shame.
You didn't listen.

The Soulless Shoe

My arms entwine
around his leg

like long shoelaces.
He peels them off.

'We've been together for only a year.'
He kicks me away.

I come running back and say,
'But I have never let you fall.'

His eyes shine just like
they used to when he

put himself inside me.
The moment passes.

He analyses me
one last time –

worn-out, weathered,
my purpose served.

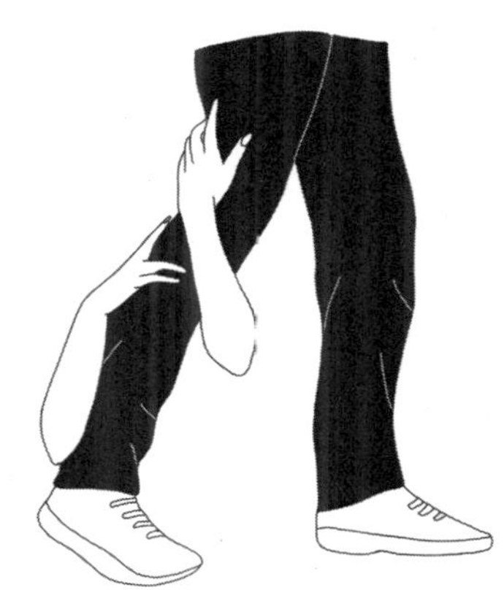

Obedience

He snatches his hand from mine.
A dictator ruling his subject.
A bully tormenting his victim.
The judge and the jury.

I am to
accept his authority,
shake like a leaf and
suffer my sentence.

The Transaction

Our home,
our room,
our books,
our memories.

Transaction completed –
his home,
his room,
his books,
my memories.

Surprisingly, his
bulky bookshelf
was carried off
effortlessly,
while I could
barely raise my ghost.

Tornado

He, a violent tornado,
wrecked my house
without warning,
destroyed all that
made it a home,

didn't even spare
a cursory glance
at the carnage
in his wake.

Memories

I accumulated my treasures
one memory at a time,
inking them in my journal.

The permanent ink
of your name on the cover
unlike you, refuses to fade.

I rip out a page,
tear it to joyless confetti,
till it matches my heart.

Then shred another
and another
and another.

But how do I
rip you
from my mind?

The Dress

My hands
trace the silver dress
you gifted
on my birthday.

Its disdain
stings my fingers.

It pines
for your touch.

It crumples
like an
empty can
in my hands.

Fleeting

The petals of the purple orchids wilting on the table.
The brown teddy bear missing its nose.
Lindt wrappers strewn on the bed.
My white dress stained with red wine.
The twenty-five-millilitre Burberry bottle losing its scent.

I should have known
our love would be next.

The Park

The park remembers
our footsteps
dancing on the grass.

Our laughter
reverberating
through the canopy.

Our kisses
swept away in the
rustling of leaves.

Our hearts
racing like cycles
on the track.

Our aspirations
rising tall
as the trees.

Our souls
soaring high like
water from fountain.

Our love
cushioning us from reality
just like the park
from its city.

Monday Blues

He makes port early morning,
explores me with a sense of urgency.

Clicks a few pictures
as though
I am an exotic capital
and he's a cruise ship,
which vows to come back
before disappearing into the sunset
to drop anchor in another harbour.

I wish
he could have stayed
a little longer
to find and fall in love with
my gruesome history
my disfigured skyline
my buried secrets
my quirky mind palace
my undiscovered sites
my adventurous vibe.

I wish
I was his home.

Lottery of Love

Lost and ______

I found myself placed in a box marked lost,
'Anyone there?'

'Stop shouting and crying.
There is no way out.
We are all worthless,'
the other forlorn articles replied.

'I don't belong here.
Help me, please.'

'Embrace it, don't make it worse.'
'I won't, there must be a way.'

Searching in a drawer,
he stopped near me –
peeled off the layer of hopelessness,
removed the debris of incompetence,
stroked my scarred skin and
polished till I was glittering.

Marvelling at his new-found treasure,
'You are perfect, mine!'

'We will keep your seat for you.'
came the call from the box.

First Date

My favourite Thai red curry loses its steam.
Droplets condense on my full margarita glass.
A couple bickers at the adjacent table.
The silverware clatters loudly.
My skin shivers from your accidental touch.

Things I unsee, lost in the world
we began creating an hour ago.

A spot of gravy blemishes my white napkin.
The flame of the table candle flickers.
The girl in the painting gazes questioningly.
I imagine beautiful fingers tracing your forehead scar.
Your hand inches away from mine.

Things I want to unsee
I want to believe again.

Lottery of Love

My heart, a beggar wrapped
in tattered memories,
pleads for spare love.
Its emptiness howls in my chest.

Is it even worth a try?

Chasing strangers –
a smile plastered across my face.
Searching for kindness, friendship,
or even a ticket in the lottery of love.

Should I even dream that big?

Expecting to be rejected again,
I tap on your window
pointing at my battered can.
You fill it to the brim.

Will you berate me if I ask for a refill?

Scared and anxious,
I knock again
the next day.
Overflow.

You have an unlimited reservoir.

Falling

He wakes me up.
Tender forehead kisses
trailing down my cheek.

My lips part to smile,
breathing his freshness and wet hair.
Abruptly, I gather the sheets

to hide my bulging stomach,
rush to the bathroom to
brush off my morning breath.

I try to snatch my sweaty hands,
'No. Not letting go.'
They sweat more as self-loathing warms them.

Collecting my broken shards in his arms,
'We will get through this.'
The unworthy fragments drift further apart.

'Periods? Getting red velvet cupcakes.'
He runs a warm bath for me on his way out.
Guilt, unlike the water, still clings on.

My favourite song plays.
He twirls and pulls me closer.
'I am so lucky.'

I push him away
and run to our room,
shutting the door behind.

My eyes unable to hold
the love I am receiving,
I weep. I weep. I weep.

Am I Enough?

He opens the door of the restaurant.
A girl walks inside, dressed in a
bodycon dress, red, his favourite colour.
Eyes hidden behind sunglasses.
Holding an LV bag on her elbow.
she points to the corner table . . .

Fingers stroke my face.
Startled, I wake up.

'Another bad dream?
You were whimpering in your sleep.'
He envelops me like a letter.
'I am here, not going anywhere.'
He whispers repeatedly like a lullaby.
I fall back asleep.

Their hands find each other across the table.
Their legs entwine under the table.

The Adhesive

I was used to
dispensing the tape of love
one pre-marked portion at a time.
Not knowing when the next
section of adhesive would be granted,
I pasted it carefully
over my deepest distress.

He sat down beside me
and opened the roll.
His fingers bled
against its sharp lines,
but he refused to give up
until I was bandaged whole.

Uber

I.

Left.
Yes.
Just keep going.
Almost there.
Will tell you when to stop.

He left before I reached my destination.
I walked the last mile on my own.

Still, I awarded a three-star rating
because I believed he had tried earnestly.

II.

It was different this time.
He asked for consent.
I flashed my lacy green.
He found his way without my GPS instructions.
Steered his tongue skilfully.
Accelerated at just the right spot.
My loud music motivated him.
My body convulsed in anticipation.
I clutched the seat belt tighter.
He kept driving.
Multiple waves crashed.

I had always dreamed of driving along
The Great Ocean Road,
Can I give ten stars?

Reading

I was sacred –
a first edition book.
He, a reader, inhaled
my sweet lingering scent
as only he could.

He placed me on the bed.
His face disappeared inside me
as he interpreted all the
mystery I offered.
Devouring me –
patiently, not wanting to miss any word,
hungrily, exploring my enigma.

Is there a perfect reading position?

He placed me in his lap.
Dived into my story.
His breathing quickened.
His heart raced.
He tried to decipher the
climax hidden in the final chapter.

Not wanting to finish –
staying with me
just a little longer –
till he had read me
the way I wanted.

If It Weren't for You

If it weren't for you
My opinions would be a boxed guitar, sitting in the corner
My resolutions would be a randomly bouncing pinball
My aspirations would be unattainable internet in early 1900s
My desires would be an unvisited cemetery
My expressions would be a black-and-white movie
My body would be an ornate, yet untouched showpiece
My creativity would be a black hole
My journey would be a shadow of my kin's
My heart would be an uninhabited ghetto
My life would be a silent recording.

If it weren't for you
Success would be a desolate destination
Endurance would be only my exam
Validation would be an unpalatable dish
Humour would be an unavailable guest
Courage would be an indecipherable text
Intimacy would be a bathroom scale
Vulnerability would be a threatening pickpocket
Happiness would be a blank diary
Love would be an unvisited museum

Long Distance

I sprint to my phone
whenever I hear your ping.
But for now
our phones stare at the ceiling unattended.
Notifications ring like hairdryers at a salon.

My fingers swipe over keys swiftly
to tell you everything.
But for now
they graze your new hairstyle,
marking my fondness on your skin.

My lips shower you with
air kisses on voice calls.
But for now
my tongue pens a
story on yours.

My eyes crave for your
blurry face on video calls.
But for now
they soak in your thinner face,
and scan the scratch on your
elbow from the accident.

My body is thousands of miles
away from yours.
But for now
It has surrendered
and is entwined with yours
not willing to or capable of letting go.

Buffet

An intoxicating drink of optimism.

Endless appetizers of care and support.

Main course of acceptance and respect,
garnished with excitement.

A cool dessert with sprinkles of kisses and hugs.

He is my buffet,
I am always hungry.

Shoes

He walks left.
I walk right.

He moves ahead.
I move backward.

We end up
walking together –
sometimes a little sideways,
sometimes a little forward –

incomplete without the other.

Wallet of Happiness

Meal Plan

Breakfast:
Pour skimmed milk in a bowl.
Add Chocos of self-doubt.
Stir till murky brown.
Consume every day.

Lunch: (A two-minute recipe)
Heat the kernels.
Hear them pop.
Scoop others' hateful opinions.
Crunch them whole.

Dinner:
Still hungry?
Grate your pessimism.
Sprinkle it like sour cheese
on the cold pizza before consuming.

Coin Toss

Heads: I shouldn't dip my toe in the ocean of happiness.
Tails: It is impossible to swim in my small pond.

Heads: 'Busy. I'll call you later.' I unpause Friends on Netflix.
Tails: After a long call, unfinished presentation stares back.

Heads: F off. You can't treat me like this.
Tails: I let her thrust the knife deeper inside me.

Heads: He remembered our anniversary when I didn't.
Tails: He didn't pick me up from the airport. He sleeps on the couch.

Heads: I fled the discounted MK store before it tempted me.
Tails: I splurged on an MK gown. Where am I going to wear it?

Heads: I am exhausted. Why did I say yes?
Tails: I wanted the project. Why did I say no?

Heads: Guilt wins.
Tails: I lose.

Guilt

The itchy bra clings to
my sweaty flesh like a
watermelon rind to its ripe fruit.
Its crescent-shaped wire cuffs my skin.

Even in solitude,
after I have discarded it,
the memory of its choking hold remains
as I stroke the grooves it leaves.

Still, I wear it
again the next day
without protest.
Why is it so normal?

Teeth

Loneliness, like the
hollow gap in my front
teeth, travels with me.

I cover my smiling lips
with my palm.
I can't divulge my
empty secret.

My tongue
like my heart,
cuts itself trying
to fill that void.

Loneliness I

Sometimes,
it is a
whack without warning.
A sharp stumble, you fall.

Sometimes,
it seems distant,
but still strikes cruelly
like a chair in the dark.

After a strong dosage of love
you walk leisurely, feeling immune,
and it stings you, like a honeybee
on a breezy summer day.

But mostly,
defenceless, you try to fight
the armed robber who strips you
of everything you hold dear.

Loneliness II

The malady that
shall not be named –
can be cured temporarily
with alcohol,
like cough with Honitus.

I wish lifetime riddance
like chickenpox
for the innocent child who
has already suffered this
dreadful disease.

Better, I wish immunity
like that provided by
polio drops,
so that no one would ever know
what this paralysing sickness feels like.

Safe

His arms hold
my shivering back.

His furry chest
soaks my tears.

His comforting closeness
warms my body.

I look up. His black
unblinking eyes understand.

I stuff another secret
into his bulging belly.

'I love you,' he bleats.
'Say that again?' I plead.

He does. My lullaby.
I straighten his bow

and fall asleep,
safe in the arms of

my brown teddy bear.

Blame

Knock knock.
The uninvited guest enters
without permission.

Why can't you drink
and enjoy losing control?

Why did you complain if
he wanted a holiday with
his friends and not you?

Why did you have to check his
phone, even when you trusted him?

Why did you switch off the TV
when he was watching a cricket match
and you wanted to go out?

Why can't you be prettier?
He wouldn't have sought anyone else.

Knock knock.
Knock knock.
No.

I lock the door.

Massage

Maybe
I am a sieve,
incapable
of holding love.

Like water,
it passes
my cracks
and flaws,

leaving only
lumps of loathing.
Heat the stones.
I place them on my spine.

y S
h c
c r
n u

Detangling them hurts.

I wish
I could hold my
dark, dull, dishevelled
thoughts in a
scrunchy
and just continue
with my day.

The Wallet of Happiness – An Advertisement

Stalked by suffering?
Fractured by failure?
Begging for bliss?

Presenting the Wallet of Happiness –
replenished monthly with
notes of laughter,
dimes of smiles and
pennies of hope.

Its hundred per cent Turkish cotton
absorbs sadness, pain and fear.

A perfect gift for family and friends.
But first, why not purchase it for self?

Visit now: www.ownhappiness.com.
First thousand orders get complimentary
yoga sessions for a month.

Christmas Bonus?
Save it with us.
Attractive offers on
debit cards.

Bankrupt?
The credit card is a
signature away.
Pay us later.

Deal of a lifetime.
Grab it now.*

*E-wallet available for
iPhone and Android.

Leaf of an Evergreen Tree

The wind whispers around me.
'See the beautiful world. Fly with me.
Glorious adventures await you.'

Please, take me.

Thunder roars,
'The wind jests. There is no paradise.
You will be reduced to ash by the world.'

No, no, there must be a way.

Meanwhile, a raindrop perches on me.
'I don't want to fall on the ground
and disappear. Carry me.'

Latch on.

The branch grips my petiole.
'Curvy margin, swollen veins, blunt blade.
You can't survive out there.'

Sway. Sway. Sway. Stay.

The wind flies away.

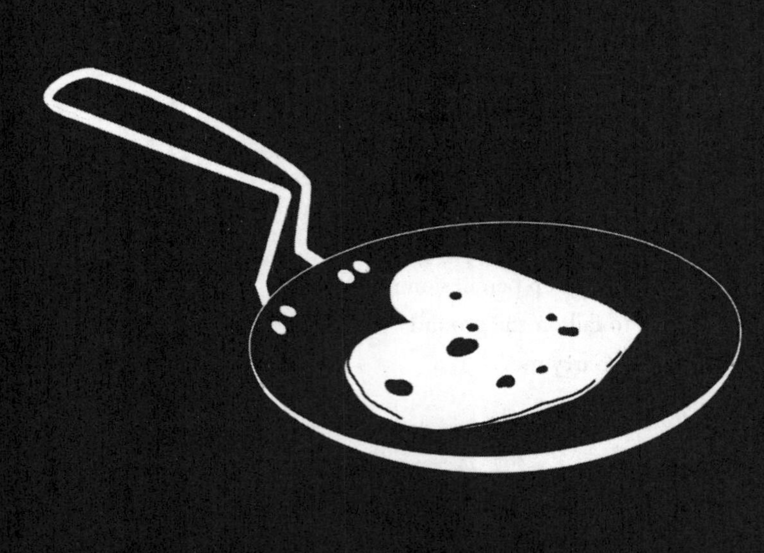

How to Do Laundry

Bloom

Gloomy thoughts
festering inside me
consume me.

Raking the withered pile,
Shredding it in anger,
I bury them deep.

The buried mulch
nourishes my mind,
A red rose sprouts in
the void left behind.

Daily

Draw
Erase

Sketch
Scratch

Colour
Smudge

Shade
Blur

Tear a version
Insert a new sheet

Paint yourself daily.

Seasons

Tears
  p p p p p
  o o o o o
  u u u u u
  r r r r r
like heavy rainfall on my
windshield. My hands refuse
to wipe off the racing droplets.

A week later –
the showers dwindle.
A light drizzle here
and

there.
Pain clings like a
barbed blanket of fog.

Memories will begin to fall
one leaf at a time
once the storm has passed.

The Cupboard

Unlatch the cupboard of your thoughts

Toss out
The T-shirt that shouts you're not enough
The skirt that keeps changing its colour
The bra that doesn't support your dreams
The shapewear that makes it difficult to breathe.

Wash
The neglected stench of bitterness
The sweat stains of sadness
The dark dirt of displeasure.

Stack
The comforting pyjamas
The jumpsuit that hugs
The breathable cotton dress
The shorts that display your beauty
The shoes that dance without a song.

Repeat periodically.

The Playlist

Skip the track of regret
Begin with the melody of acceptance
Increase the volume of laughter
Rewind to the past, but only to learn
Forward self-doubt
Mute others' opinions
Sing your song louder.

Overcome?

A dark solemn night –

Water, like tears, poured
from the sky steadily.
Thunder, like anger,
struck repeatedly.
Warmth, like happiness,
seemed far away.
Stars, like hope in my heart,
fluttered dully.

The flood of misery was
drowning my canoe.

Rescue me!
No one came,
Have mercy,
None was granted.

One last try,
Despite the pain,
I paddled against the
strong current of adversity,
colliding brutally with the
large waves of misfortune.

I just have to stay afloat,

The scent of land
called out to me like
food to a famished stomach.

The sun rose behind me.
My wet feet cherished the dry sand.

Perspective

I.

It was raining yesterday.
Umbrellas fought with one another
as I crossed the street.
My cheek cut.
A car splashed a puddle.
My squelchy shoes criss-crossed
other brown footprints
as I reached my office desk.
Ladies' Room – I lifted my dress
to the hand dryer machine.
Another girl opened the door.
A colleague stared at
my nude underwear.

II.

Today, it is raining again.
Office – I put my waterproof coat in a plastic bag.
My trousers don't cling to my skin.
The notes dry in my laptop compartment.
Raindrops tap my glass window.
A greener tree waves at me.
I walk to the conference room
armoured with my laptop and bare belief.
Later, the smell of pakoras wafts
in the office air, I dip mine
in ketchup and sip my warm tea.
Outside, I put my paper boat in
the puddle. It sails.

How to Do Laundry

My family finds me
spread on the floor of my room.

Torn apart by breakup,
faded by monotonous work,
stained with self-loathing,
speckled with hopelessness,
unzipped resilience.

Presoaked in love,
I am spun with understanding.

Unblemished,
I am tumbled in warmth.

Uncreased.
Stitched one piece at a time.

I am a beautiful dress again.

Ring! Ring! Ring!

You called at 12.05 on my birthday.
I wish these were bigger.
Did you fake it?
You're wearing THIS?
Writing is not going to pay bills.
My mom thinks you're selfish.
You're such a princess.
I can't take care of you.

Again.
He rings.
I pick up.

I cut off mid-sentence.

Silence.

My words travel to me.
An affirmation at a time.

Bolder

I tried to
heave,
pivot,
roll,
disintegrate,
pray.

But the bulky black boulder
of heartbreak didn't budge.

I can't let it win.

I drilled a hole in the boulder
piercing as deep as my hurt.

I placed the chisel of my regret in the cavity and
hammered it with all the rage I had stored.

The boulder cracked open – two halves.

I pushed the blocks.
They tumbled down the stairs –
reduced to black pebbles.

His indifferent eyes looked at me,
I kicked them away.

Therapist

I'm not a robust chair.
My arms feel wobbly.

My back contorts.
Fear unpicks my seams.

Anger, like a termite,
consumes me.

Anxiety, like a prickly stole,
tightens its grip around me.

Blissful thoughts are
as rare as resting cats.

Grief stacks like worn clothes.
My legs unable to hold the load,

I look for someone to repair me.
He strips my old fabric,

replaces my crumbling foam
and stitches me back.

He understands me.
I understand love.

He's my mender.

Befriend the Darkness

Loneliness, like darkness,
is consuming and endless.

The monster stares.

I scream loudly.
I kick frantically.
I pray faithfully.

'You are alone,' it laughs.

Slowly,
Hours pass, maybe days.
Fear walks away.
Anxiety stands in the corner.
My breath returns to me.

I befriend the darkness.

How to Make Cutting Chai

Boil loneliness and sadness. Add
one cube of unreciprocated love and
grated ginger guilt.
Crush the seeds of rage. Sprinkle them.
Put two teaspoons
of anxiety. Stir until black.

Brew, brew, brew.

Add half cup of pure white happiness.

Pour boiling tea
from the kettle
i
n
t
o
the cUp
of your journal.

Breathe in the
glorious
aroma of life.

Saturday Night for an Introvert

Date night for parents.
Sibling leaves with friends.

I change into my bathrobe,
sprinkle lavender salts into my pool.

The lullaby of pouring
water soothes my anxiety.

My dull aching body
surrenders to the warmth.

My eyes settle under the mask.
The hair on my legs bristles with excitement.

My lover holds me.
I am born again.

Love for an Introvert

I am not a glass door.
I expect you to walk away
because you can't see through me.

Only a few people would be
fascinated with a
solid wooden door.

Surprisingly, you're still observing.
My planks are scratched.
Dark lines run through them
like varicose veins.
A few patches are unpolished.
My letterbox protrudes
like a bulging stomach.

I shut my spectacled peephole
when you catch me staring back.

You tap to find hollow spots
inside my heart, and say,
'I love how you're hinged
to your imperfections.
They define you.'

And that was the 'Alohomora'
I needed – my lock unlatches.

A Toast to Introverts

To being called shy, docile and soft-spoken.

To not letting words escape our tongues
despite them bouncing like pinballs in our heads.

To not letting our volcanic emotions erupt through our mouths.

To always being the listener.

To searching for and finding peace in our cosy lair that allows entry for one.

To avoiding confrontations.

To cringing at the question – how are you?

To unrolling the yarn of our thoughts in our journals.

To keeping our hands down despite knowing the answer.

To borrowing the world of the book we are reading and living in it.

To solitude.
To me.
To you.
To us.

My Room

I want
A wardrobe that hangs my uncreased happiness
A drawer that stores my despair, do not open
A dustbin where I toss my anger
A shredder for guilt
A shelf that displays trophies of resilience
A desk where I mull over my fears
A painting that covers my scars
A corner to read solitude
A mirror that accepts
A sink to wash away self-doubt
A bleach bottle for anxiety
Windows that see but don't covet
A bookshelf of experience
A shower of love
A tap of flowing support
I want my room.

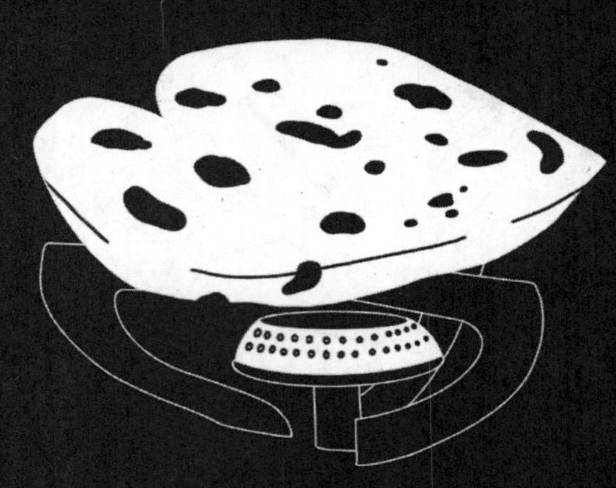

The Indian Matchmaker

Death Knell

Twenty-five? Older?
Unmarried?
Girl?

Distinguished degrees discarded
like scribbled sketches
from childhood.

Dainty neck barren
without a mangalsutra
woven around it.

Reputation branded, as if with
a permanent pustule, proliferating
as the months shamelessly roll into a year.

Parents endure condolences,
their heads heavy with remorse
as the death knell of her worth is tolled.

She fasts for sixteen consecutive Mondays.
Still, the promised husband
doesn't appear.

What Was Said When He Fell in Love

She can't even cook okra
She drinks tequila
Look! This guy is hugging her on Facebook
Short skirts. Hot pants –
that's all she's wearing
She likes her job more than you

You're innocent
I have seen the world

Your love won't last
Promises won't be kept

You have had your fun
I only care about you and your happiness
I will choose someone for you.

What Was Said When She Fell in Love

He drives a Honda
He has been in the same company since the last five years
You will just be shifting from one rented house to another
My astrologer assured me that you would rule a business empire

Leave him

I only care about you and your happiness.

Stop crying. I will find someone for you.

His Requirements for Bride

I want someone

young because she will be fearful
fair because only that's beautiful
untouched because otherwise it's sinful
homely because that's useful
pliable because arguments are unfruitful
dolled up because that's lustful
traditional because my mind would be peaceful
loving because my joy is meaningful
affluent because my life would be plentiful.

For I am a prince
and I will have the perfect girl.

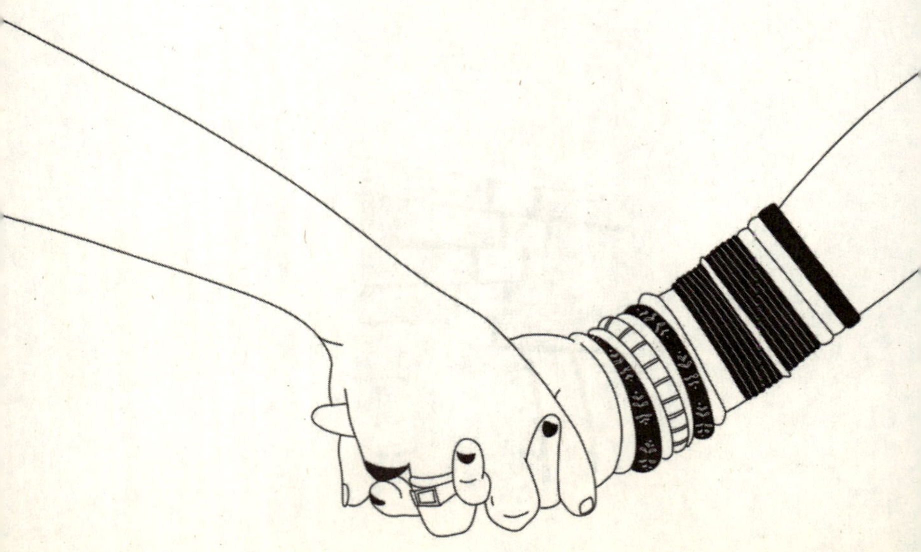

Her Requirements for Groom

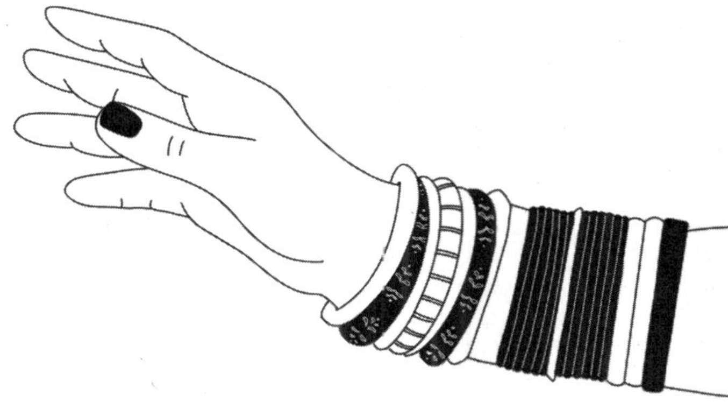

Panditji

He's sitting on a pedestal.
Parents queue – folded hands, bowed heads.

I.

(Looking at the kundalis*)
18/36 guna** match.
They score high on health and prosperity.

The first meeting, it wasn't good?
That happens.
They'll be amicable after marriage.

Kanya mangalik*** hai.
Don't change her time of birth.
I will perform a kumbh vivah.

Your girl will be happy.
Jai Shri Ram.
(Parents touch Panditji's feet and leave.)

---

* (Hindi) Horoscope charts created for matchmaking.
** (Hindi) Points allocated to the couple on how well they match for marriage according to the horoscope of both candidates.
*** (Hindi) A mangalik bride will cause her husband's early death.

II.

You have found a heera.
30/36 guna match.
Business will prosper.
Children will be healthy.

No, they will live with you.
No, she won't control your son.
She's not an abomination.
She will get along with your wife.

Yes,
arrange the meet-up.
Jai Shri Ram.
(Father touches Panditji's feet and leaves.)

III.

Give me the rice.
Kept it under your pillow at night?

(Strokes rice in palms)
You like to WORK?
You are an introvert?
You studied abroad?
You're not eager to marry?
(nods)

Date of birth?
(I reply)

Shani bhari hai.
Wear black, donate black sesame, every Saturday.
Hanuman chalisa every morning.
Solitaire diamond ring, pinkie finger, left hand.

Marriage is next to next year.
(stifled sobs)

Don't be stubborn, beti.
Sab kuch kisi ko nahin milta.

Coins?
(One gold, two silver handed,
chants mantra, returns silver)

Keep these in your purse.
Jai Shri Ram.

www.indianmatchmaker.com

In India, marriage is a union between two families, not just two souls.
That is why we help you and your kin find your perfect life partner.
One million satisfied parents in just ten years.

To find your beautiful, well-cultured and family-oriented bride, click here.
Speaks: Hindi/Punjabi/Tamil/Gujarati/Marathi
Complexion: Aishwarya/Deepika
Height: (Hint– she shouldn't reach your level)
Weight: Slim/Hourglass
Eyesight: Normal/LASIK
Eating habits* : Indian/Chinese/Thai
Education: Asks before planning to go out/Informs before going out/Feminist**
Age: Intact hymen/Broke while cycling
My worth***: Wedding/Wedding + sedan/Wedding + Audi+ 3 BHK
Loading bride...

---

*These options reflect her cooking capabilities.
** If you selected this, our service is not for you.
*** To access our dowry calculator click here.

To find your provider, click here.

Speaks: Hindi/Punjabi/Tamil/Gujarati/Marathi

Family Income: Flat/Beach House

Shareholders: One brother/Only son

City: Please check– I am willing to relocate for my husband.

My budget***: Engineer/IIT/IIT+IIM/Industrialist family

Loading groom...

The Indian Matchmaker

I.

No, no. Newspaper ads aren't reliable.
No, no. Love marriages end in divorce.

I will find the perfect match for your son.

Yes, Check this one –
girl from Garg family.
You haven't heard of them?
That's surprising.
Similar family background.
Down-to-earth people.

Look at her photo, so graceful in a sari.
Zoom in, she even has dimples.
Adorable, isn't it?

She is an angel.
Didn't say a thing.
She cooks Thai also.
Isn't that your favourite cuisine, beta?

No, no, she doesn't want to work.
Her US MBA was very hectic.
She will take care of you
while you conquer the world, beta.

This profile came in yesterday.
You are the first family to see this.
I have a good feeling.
When should I schedule the meet-up?

II.

No, no. Marriage.com is unreliable.
No, no. References from family and friends are limited.

I will find the perfect match for your daughter.

His family has a jewellery showroom
in Greater Kailash. They opened another just for him.

Yes, yes, it is doing well.
He's already earning in eight figures.

Yes, I saw their house –
his parents on ground,
he's on first,
has a jacuzzi,
a well-equipped gym,
his and her bathrooms,
a four-poster bed.
Honestly, it's a palace,
They also have a farmhouse in Chattarpur.

Well, they just want a simple destination
wedding at a palace in Udaipur.
You know how it is – three hundred of
their close friends and family.
Just a little something to make memories.
That's in your budget, right?
Oh, I forgot to tell you,
the elder sister is already married.
So, everything belongs to him only.

His mom is very religious –
she matched kundalis,
liked your daughter from there.

I have scheduled for Thursday at 4 p.m.,
next week, works?

III.

The families meet up at a poolside restaurant.

The potential life partners
are permitted to discuss their
future at a nearby table.

The girl sips water.

The guy places his leg on his knee,
'What are your hobbies?'

The girl replies, 'Swimming and dancing.'

'I don't like dancing that much,
but there is a famous dance
studio near our house.'

'That's amazing.'

Roka ceremony performed after lunch.

Marriage finalized –
six months to the date.

My Big Fat Indian Wedding

Begin dance rehearsals
a month before the wedding.

Distract me.

The gold-plated invitations look exquisite.

His friends would be my friends.

Dangle the Sabyasachi lehenga.

I will resign from work after marriage.

Showcase the jewellery from the
latest Bhansali movie –
the one that Queen Deepika wore.

His home is my home.

The exotic Udaipur hotel is
available for my wedding dates.

Graciously honour the life my
mother-in-law picks for me.

Intricate henna applied on my hands.
His name shines in dark red.

Thank God, my husband will love me.
I am a success story.

Wedding will be the most
special day of your life.

Walking down the aisle in reality,
why do I want to throw up?

Kanyadan

I.

Folded hands.
Bowed bodies.

The parents gave away
the beautiful red package,
adorned in gold
to its rightful owners.

Along with
an extravagant ceremony,
and a premium car.

Rules obeyed to the letter –
her parents have repaid their
debt to the universe.

II.

The parents gave their heart.

Hoping their daughter
would gain what the
traditions promised –

happiness, safety,
children and love.

They return home –
a home that was never hers.

Passport

From the throng of pretty dolls –
all dressed in intricate red lehengas –

he picks me.
Checks the weight

of my gold case before
swaggering ahead

in a navy blue sherwani.
Opens the next level with his master key.

Collars the mangalsutra around my neck,
holding the leash.

'On your knees.'
Stamps sindoor on my forehead.

'Sign your submission form.
NO. Your new name.'

We head towards the exit.
Outside. My breath returns to me.

I touch his parents' feet.
Society embraces me.

'Carry your visa and stamp at all times.'
I nod. I raise my medal and touch it to my lips.

Arranged Marriage

My parents enrolled me in a
chaotic, consuming, customary course.
Love was not a prerequisite –
a postscript, maybe.

Lectures with mother-in-law began –

Moral Science:
Wake up before him
Prepare breakfast, pack lunch
Leave for work
Welcome him home
Ask him about his day.

History:
His father established an empire
because I stayed at home.

Geography:
Plan a trip to Vaisho Devi –
pray for the good health of your husband,
pray for obedient children.

Biology:
Clock is ticking
Preferably mornings
Preferably facing east
Preferably a boy.

Physics:
Every action doesn't have an equal
and opposite reaction.
Tolerate, suppress, forget.

Complimentary cooking classes:
He loves okra.

Report card sent to my parents:
Needs frequent reminders to be attentive.
Physics seems difficult to grasp.
Late with her Biology assignment.
Scope for improvement.

How do I
graduate with Honours
in a course I didn't want to take?

A Sunday Brunch

His friends look expectantly
in our direction, he clasps my frozen fingers.
'This is my wife. I picked this dress for her,
doesn't she look gorgeous?'
I brush my dress softly.

He pecks my cheek, claims,
'She started her own lifestyle brand.
Doing well, her hours longer than mine,
but weekends are prohibited.'
He caresses my back, I flinch.

'You must visit our home.
She selected an oil painting. A gem.
Exorbitantly priced, but
anything to make HER happy.'
My lips widen.

'She and my mother
are best friends,
brave feminist women.'
I blink my eyes rapidly
to absorb their wetness.

Walk back to our car –
He drops my hand.
'Cancel meetings for tomorrow. Vermas
are coming for lunch. Wear something
suitable. I can't help you every day.'

At home,
'Fuck, that girl's gaze is terrifying –
good *you* paid for that monstrosity.
Throw it in the storeroom.'
He pours Scotch in his den,
shuts his door loudly.

I am sitting on my dresses,
strewn like my sadness.
His mom calls me downstairs
to hear about the brunch,
'You're so lucky to have my son.'

The Switch

I am a modern
suspended light –
sculpted to perfection,
showcased to my society.

Bound by a cable –
I seem to fly in the air
like a fearless bird.
But my wings are made of glass.

I could illuminate an entire room
but I am not expected
to be anything more than
a decoration,

Expected to turn on
whenever my husband desires.

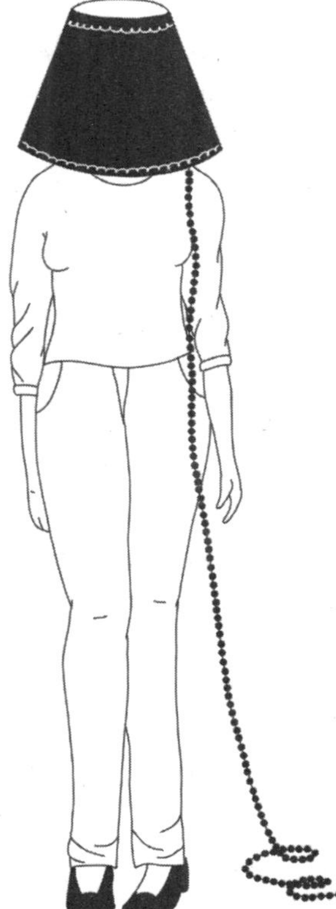

Remembering Childhood

My father would nod at me
only if
I stood first in class.
Now,
I should be the first of my friends
to become a Mrs.

I used to wander
the toy store for hours
till I found my perfect Barbie.
But now,
a Ken doll has been
arranged for me.
I should behave
as he instructs.

Drugged with coffee,
I worked until my eyes dried
to be the lucky one at my job.
But now,
I walk seven times
around the consecrated fire
because the astrologer
assured my new parents
I would be auspicious.

Even peeking
at liquor was prohibited.
But now,
on my wedding night
the wine bottle is thrust inside me –
I should stain the sheets red.

When I was ten, I asked,
'What do you dream about, Ma?'
She replied,
'My child should be safe and happy,
You are my everything,'
I laughed.

But now,
her dainty palms touch my chest,
my breasts quiver as she sucks –
I can't fail my daughter!

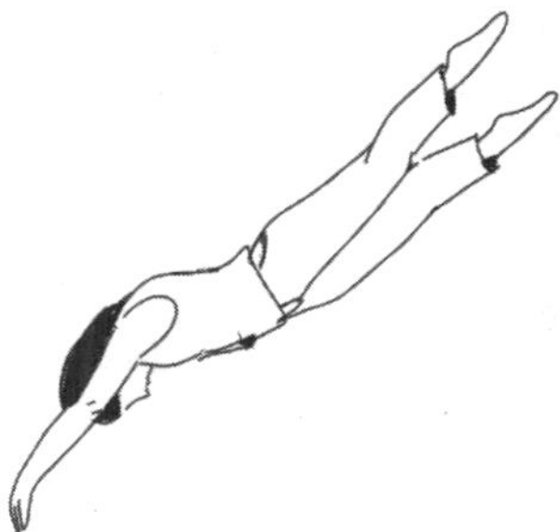

A Woman's Lexicon

How to Make Round Rotis

Snatch the book she is reading intently.
Pull her hand, her weight if you have to.
Assemble the bowls and ingredients.
Hit her with the rolling pin if she refuses.

'This is for your own good,'
assure her periodically.

Take two cups of unbound flour in a mixing bowl.
Add three-fourth cup of water of discontentment.
Knead with knuckles of fragile hands.
Reiterate, the dough should be
soft, smooth and pliable.
Touch floured hand to forehead, make it white.

Remove a dream from the dough.
Roll on hands until it is confined to a circle.
Place on the rolling board and crush (lightly).
Use ingrained displeasure and rage to
flatten it with a rolling pin.
Toss the roti on the virtuous tawa.

Round and puffed,
serve it warm for a worthy fortune.

Protect Her

Reading can kill
Traditional thoughts might evaporate
Dark clouds of opinion might gather
Lightning questions might strike
Thunderous debates might follow
She shouldn't be drenched in knowledge
She shouldn't write her story
It has been cast in stone, for generations.

Painting is injurious to health
She might observe the intricacies
of people around her.
She might adorn the canvas
with her personality
and immortalize her name.
She shouldn't bare her deepest desires
She shouldn't mould her destiny
It has been prophesied for generations.

Being at home every day keeps death away
Gates of opportunity might open
Her energy might be sufficient
to turn the turbines of success.
She shouldn't be independent
She shouldn't be a powerhouse
She's been a tarnished machine for generations.

She is
a blank book
a chaste canvas
a desireless dependant.

Ensure she stays that way.
Always.

A Woman's Lexicon

When I first stained my underwear
red, my grandmother told
'You are a woman now.
This is your dictionary.'

Ambition: selfish
Beautiful: fair
Career: hobby
Descendant: mandatory
Education: prerequisite for a wealthy husband
Femininity: docile, incapable and sacrificing
Girl: the only gender of friends allowed
Hair: ugly (except eyebrows and scalp)
Independence: results in rape
Joke: smile, don't tell
Kitchen: workplace
Lust: unnatural
Menstruation: entry prohibited to kitchen, temple and rooms
Night (sunset): stay at home
Opinion: refer father/husband
Pray: to Lord Ram every day that men aren't tempted by you
Rape: is always your fault
Sin: losing innocence
Time: enemy, beauty fades
Underclothes: should never be visible
Vodka: never. Leads to rape

Whisper: your permissible volume
Xerox: mom, mother-in-law
Yes: the only admissible answer
Zen: serve parents and husband

My arms wrapped around my stomach
trying to mollify the pain. She pulled them apart.
'Back straight. Smile. Yes.'

Catcall, Attack, Harass

My Mama says:
What a man wants. A man grabs.

At a vacant park, a chap stalks:
Baby, why stay far apart?
Baby. Smack. Mwah. Baby. Smack. Mwah.

A starry sky and a small walkway.
Wham! A hand slaps my ass and darts.

A bald brawny nawab brags at a bar:
Want a daft arm candy? Want tasty pasta? Want a warm sack?
Marry! Marry! Marry!

At an art hall, a lanky chap draws
and cracks: Damn! That's a flat rack.

At a mall, a black Mazda halts,
blasts rampant horn, starts a jam, that man yawps:
Talk. Hang. Crash at my flat.

At a day camp, a pal yanks
my hand, plants on hard pants.

My Mama warns:
Can't thwart that scary alpha. Can't act angry. Can't attack back.
March. Scat. Dash.

Hair

I didn't inherit
this disease from Mama.
She is pure,
soft smooth skin.

Papa exhibits symptoms,
But he is respected and suave.

Why am I the cursed one?

Weeds sprout on my skin.
Proliferate in directions unknown.

Chant repeatedly –
'The black beasts
must be neutralized.'

Options:Promises
Razor (lubricated with aloe extract): no nicks
Epilator:four weeks of peace
Chocolate wax:painless transition
Depilatory cream:no chemical burns

Even if they don't keep their promises,
I have to keep mine –
I have to be a girl.

Don't Detest, Loathe, Despise

The maroon stain your XL pad couldn't soak
The red satin noodle strap dress that embraces you, as a lover should
The dark defiant soldiers that refused to be waxed
The bronze medal that won't turn to gold
The career you want to nurture as your baby
The disagreements with loved ones justifying your dreams
The carnal desire you would rather not open
Your body that limps sometimes but walks again.

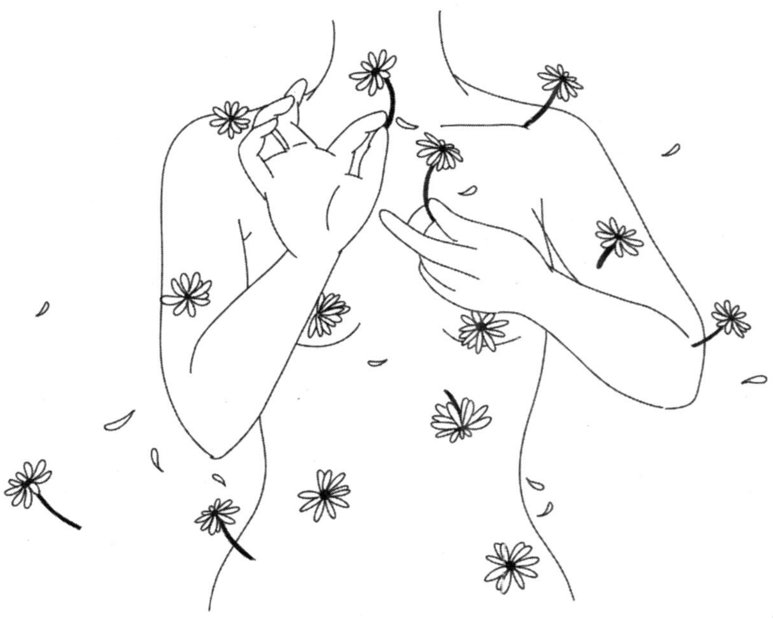

Lust

It hits –
a tiny flick,
an indistinct wish,
a shy inkling.
Things switch within.
Dismiss it.
It is sick and evil.

Third strike –
it visits with a ringing hiss.
Its spirit trying to stir my
spirit with grit.
I fight.
It exits.

Fifth blitz –
I sprint to ditch
the slimy glitch.

Ninth stint –
striding with rigidity,
it lights my mind.
Its thirst mimicking the
rapidly rising itch within.
Fright dwindling.
The spinning whirlwind
whips my misgivings.

It is wild & still.
It is thrilling & sinking.
It is intrinsic.
It is BLISS.

The First Time, and Every Time After

Wrap in customised cling film
before it enters your sacred room.

Stop if you aren't comfortable.
Stop if you've changed your mind.
Stop if you're not ready.
Stop if it's paining.

You are yours to grant access.
It is your choice.

Labels

I watch them
label me

Informed: DWEEB
Ignorant: DITSY

Yes: WHORE
No: BITCH

Skintight short skirt: SLUT, SHUNNED
Oversized outfit: UGLY, UNLOVABLE

Achiever: FEMINIST
Asleep: TROPHY

Fat: PREGNANT
Thin: ANOREXIC

Single: TRAMP
Married: WIFEY

I place their labels on a strip of paper.
Roll. Seal. Light. Puff.

Their words disappear in
wisps of smoke.

PMS

The monthly visitor
sends regards before

her ominous arrival, triggering a
domino effect of chaos.

Despairing thoughts
honk in my head.

Unable to find a parking spot,
I slap the steering wheel repeatedly.

My hands embrace my
stomach to caress the pain.

My cramped limbs
seek sympathy in sleep.

My aching back begs
the seat for support.

Despair washes down my face.
Maybe I don't even deserve a space.

A throbbing fatigue infects my body.
I brace myself for her arrival.

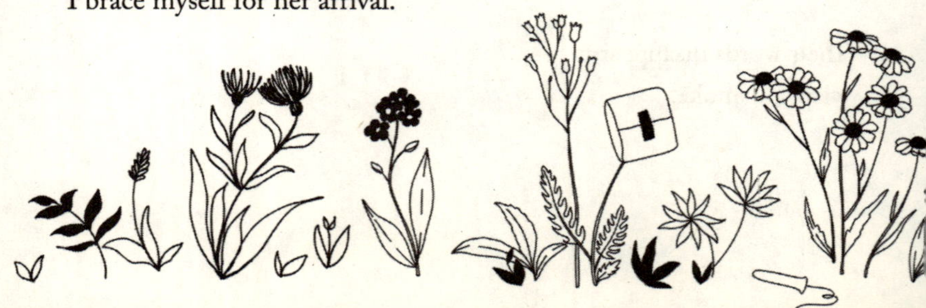

Periods

Unpredictability, her trademark.
Sometimes a day early.
Sometimes a couple of days late.

No bells ring.
The guest arrives at
her convenience.

I switch from dresses to trousers.
My bulging stomach refusing
to be contained in the seams.

I grab products and medicines
from my bag, hasten to make her
stay as painless as possible.

I examine, re-examine
chairs and cushions as we move from
one place to another.
A rigorous exercise that proves futile.

Unpredictability, her trademark.
Sometimes stays a couple of days.
Sometimes a week.

'Less uproar next time?
Shall we fix a date?'
We both enjoy a hearty laugh.

She bids farewell.

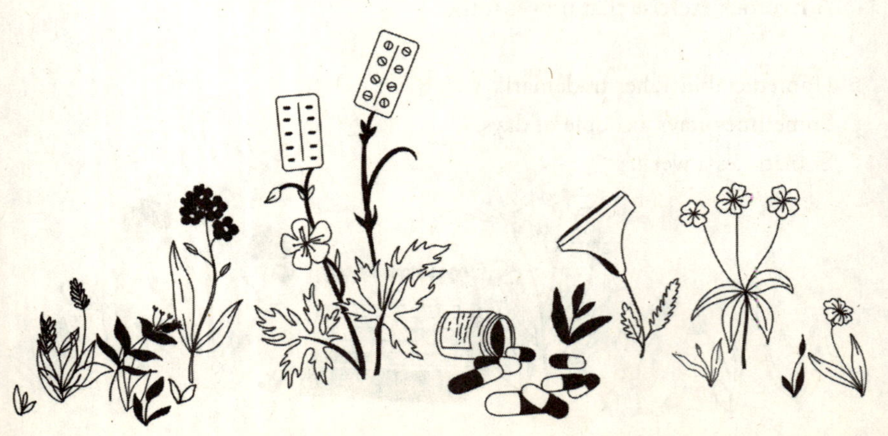

Late

The portentous application on my phone beeps.
The visitor is due today. But my panties are white.

Granted, I might have tried
a couple of positions that weren't
entirely easy, but what lacked in comfort
made up in joy and satisfaction.
I slept with a sweet smile
that soul-satisfying night.

Unable to focus on impending
deadlines at work, my own deadlines unmet,
I google reasons for delay –.
Would throwing my laptop on the floor,
stomping on it repeatedly, reduce stress?
A work call begins, a breakdown averted.

A day seems like a year.
One step away from disintegrating –
I google 'how to induce periods'.
I meditate. Go for a run. Cry my worries out.
Drink ginger tea. Eat papaya, kiwi, carrot,
saunf, jeera, ajwain.

When his words don't work,
his mouth calms me down.
I peak. Again.
Come on Google!
I am trying everything here.

Two years elapse.
I vow not to poke my
sacred room for a month.
Three years elapse.
Shall I get a test kit. Tomorrow, maybe.

When I get up the next morning,
my underwear is red.
My hands shake uncontrollably
as I text him –
Pineapple.

His sigh is louder than mine,
unlike the night we were together.

How to Write a Feminist Bestseller

Introduce a docile,
yet intelligent,
girl.

Choose an ethnic minority
or better, set it in a war zone.
Critical acclaim.

Bullies only,
no friends.
Reader relates.

She smuggles books.
The patriarch drains alcohol.
Reader cringes.

Mistreat. Beat. Repeat.
Still, dreams refuse to bleed from her wounds.
Reader cries.

A saviour swings, buys ice cream of freedom.
She licks it once, the clock strikes midnight.
Reader hopes.

He promises her 'a happily ever after'.
Consent given. Clothes discarded.
Reader shouts with joy.

Remorseful,
she runs away.
Leave it at that?

Or trembling,
she wakes up.
Her owners have found her.

Maybe it's a dream. Maybe not.
The end.
The reader will drink every book you pour.

The Anthem

Tear the traditions that
demand acceptance
without questions.

They might call you a *slut*
for showing your ankles.
They might even brand you
the dirty word *rebel*
or even worse *feminist*
for daring to decide your destiny.
Wear it like a gold star.

Burn your lungs. Roar.
Till it becomes an anthem –
A voice that cannot be muffled
A body that denies defeat
A grit that's pure WOMAN.

Outlandish Aspirations

I can't walk but I want to run.
I can't articulate but I want to write.
I can't float but I want to swim.
I can't make friends but I want to fall in love.
I can't break even but I want profits.
I can't smile but I want to be laugh.
I can't reflect but I want to shine.

But I remember yesterday –
I couldn't stand.
I couldn't think originally.
I couldn't get over aquaphobia.
I couldn't find anyone to talk to.
I couldn't sell.
I couldn't stop crying.
I couldn't be polished.

I can,
I want to,
I will.

I Drive

My intuitive GPS
displayed low congestion,
but here I am
stuck in a gridlock.

A cycle breezes by.
I am green. Inside.
Outside. I am red.

Inspired,
I polish my imperfections,
I fuel up on courage,
I turn on the ignition,
I am on a highway.

Barricade!
I come to a screeching halt.
Unwilling to reverse, I fume.
My 'check uncertainty' light blinks away,
I see 'Persevere' stamped on a billboard,
I recalibrate and reach my checkpoint.

Meanwhile, a few cars honk,
'Get out, you don't belong here,
you're despicable and defective.'
I clean my mucky windscreen
I increase my morale volume and
I enjoy the serene scenery.

The journey seems daunting,
but my HUD looks heartening,
my number plate beaming,
I continue driving.

PS: An accidental glance
in my rear-view mirror
paints a picture of my past,
The start sign is now a speck.

Art

A blank page can be an
abomination for many.

Only a select few
rise up to the challenge.

Draw daring dreams on their canvas
placed on the easel of time.

Paint with colours of
diligence, perseverance and hope.

The glorious art is
then framed by Destiny,

Before it is hung in the Museum
of Accomplishments like a Medal of Honour.

— Epilogue —

One Door Closed

I.

Once, I had a vision
of my life after half a century:
dream fulfilled of leading a
successful start-up –
probably the only child I parented, now graduated –
I'd relinquish my responsibilities
to nurture my passion.
My knees unable to run due to
a disease that runs in my family.
I'd read. I'd write. I'd read. I'd write.
Devouring books, I sit near the window
overlooking my tree, my hands scribbling
on the yellowed pages of the journal
I purchased when I was eighteen.
I'd write. I'd write. I'd write. I'd write.

II.

A year after my quarter-century,
symptoms appeared gradually.
The discomfort and pain in my knee
rose month after month.
My start-up starting to stand up
and walk, doctors recommended a surgery
if I desired to do the same. My swollen knee
had crippled both of us. Teary-eyed and shaken,
I cut off the oxygen of investment.
Confined to my bed, I forced myself to breathe.
I read, inhaling books like they were air.
Writing came gradually –
one scattered breath at a time.

Slowly, the words held each other.
Their strength battling against
the melancholy set in my soul.

My book might release this fall.
Never before have I been an overachiever.

– Notes –

Gratitude to the following journals for publishing versions of the poems appearing in this book:

The American Journal of Poetry, 'Arranged Marriage'
Magma Poetry, 'Passport'
One Art Poetry, 'First Prize' (published as 'The Trophy'), 'What Was Said When He Fell in Love', 'What Was Said When She Fell in Love' and 'Swimming Pool'
Sky Island Journal, 'Leaf of an Evergreen Tree'
Madras Courier, 'Remembering Childhood'
ANGLES, 'Bully'
Visual Verse, 'My Big Fat Indian Wedding'
For Woman Who Roar, 'How to make Round Rotis'
Green Hills Literary Lantern, 'Privilege'
The Punch Magazine, 'The Bottle of Promises', 'Seasons', 'The Transaction', 'Reading', 'My Room'
Muse (India), 'Ice Lolly Recipe' (published as 'How to Prepare an Ice Lolly'), 'Panditji', 'A Restaurant Monologue', 'Fly' and 'Death Knell'
The Alipore Post (India), 'The Couch'
Dreich Magazine & Press (Scotland), 'Kanyadan' , 'My Façade' and 'Catcall, Attack, Harass'
Drawn to the Light Press, 'Lullaby'
Pure Slush (Australia), 'Periods'
Ariel Chart, 'My Crowned Childhood'

'The Switch' (Published as 'Decoration'), 'Labels', 'Protect Her' and 'A Woman's Lexicon' (published as 'Lexicon') were shortlisted for the The Woman Inc. & Beyond Black Sakhi Annual Poetry Awards 2019. A few poems were also shortlisted for the Cinnamon Press Literature Award 2020.

– Acknowledgements –

Thank you to my parents for their unending love, support and inspiration. Hope this makes them proud. Special thanks to my brother, Mohak Goyal, for encouraging and pushing me to write this book.

Thank you to the Juggernaut Team: Chiki Sarkar and Arani Sinha. A special thanks to Chiki, who had faith in my writing. This book wouldn't have been possible without you.

Thank you to Naomi Foyle who read all my poems and made this book better in every way.

Thank you to my illustrator Shikhar Gaur for his countless iterations of the black-and-white drawings in the book. He has added another dimension with his brilliance, innovative and clever drawings.

Thank you to Meena Rajasekaran for her generous advice and amazing formatting. The book looks better than I could have imagined.

Thank you to my best friend Tara. I wouldn't have started writing if it weren't for her. She held my hand and showed me the way.

Thank you to Michelle for being my mentor and introducing me to the magical world of poetry.

Thank you to Anjann Singh for pushing me to write my (hesitant yet loud) heart out, helping me edit the poems, finalise the title and shape the book.

Thank you Deepthi Chandran, Keya, Uttara Poddar, Yaju Gupta, Mahima Razdan, Saloni Rajpal, Sakshi Raj, Ritesh Gupta, Gautam Gupta and Shourya Raj Gupta, for being my constant cheerleaders. Special thanks to Tamanna Dhamija for inspiring me and believing in me.

Thank you Anand Neelkanthan, Rohan Monteiro and Arcopol Chaudhuri for the much-needed advice and support especially when I was lost.

Thank you to Sachin for his unfailing faith in the book. And in me.

Thank you to everyone else whom I have met, who has influenced me and who has been there.

– A Note on the Author –

Mehak Goyal was a computer science engineer and start-up founder before committing herself to writing. This is her first book. She lives in Chandigarh.

Website: www.mehakgoyal.com
Instagram: @mehakgoyal.poetry
Facebook: f/poetrybymehak
Twitter: @poetic_quill